Presenting
secrets

The experts tell all!

About the author
Martin Manser BA (Hons), MPhil teaches communication skills at the London College of Communication. He is a language trainer and consultant, and also a reference book editor. Among his books is *Time Management*, also in the **business secrets** series.

Author's note
Thank you to Alfred Biehler, Michael and Jeanette Hulcoop, Tim Duffy, Hannah and Brian Murphy.

Presenting
secrets

Collins
A division of HarperCollins*Publishers*
77-85 Fulham Palace Road, London W6 8JB

www.BusinessSecrets.net

First published in Great Britain in 2010 by HarperCollins*Publishers*
Published in Canada by HarperCollins*Canada*. www.harpercollins.ca
Published in Australia by HarperCollins*Australia*. www.harpercollins.com.au
Published in India by HarperCollins*PublishersIndia*. www.harpercollins.co.in

1

Copyright © HarperCollins*Publishers* 2010

Martin Manser asserts the moral right to be identified as the author of this work.

A catalogue record for this book is available from the British Library.

ISBN 978-0-00-732447-7

Printed and bound at Clays Ltd, St Ives plc

Contents

Learn how to give the perfect presentation

We give presentations to provide information, explain something, present choices, sell a product or service, or persuade others to follow a course of action. Unfortunately, presentations can be dull. But yours doesn't have to be. I've written this book to guide you through every step of the preparation so that your presentation communicates your message effectively and is successful.

My natural temperament is to be shy. Being the youngest of four children meant that I was a listener and generally kept my thoughts to myself. Gradually over the years I've come out of my shell and had the courage to express myself. Actually, it's been a long and at times difficult struggle – and at times I've wanted to say something in a larger group but haven't been brave enough to do so.

I've been giving presentations on various subjects for many years now and have gradually become less nervous and more confident. So I want to share with you some of the tips, hints and techniques that I've learnt the hard way.

This book consists of 50 **secrets** of giving good presentations, divided into seven chapters:

■ **Prepare the basics.** If you have a clear idea of your audience and what you want to tell them, you are already on the way to success.

■ **Work on your words.** You need to spend time refining your key messages to make sure they are clear.

■ **Plan for props and other people.** Good use of visual aids can make a huge impact. A picture really can speak a thousand words.

■ **Prepare your mind.** Positive thinking makes a positive difference. It's normal to be nervous; you don't need to be afraid of fear.

■ **Interact with your audience.** Remember you're giving a presentation, not a speech. An effective dialogue with the audience will ensure that you are giving them what they want.

■ **Be aware of body language.** Research has shown that body language is an important factor in a successful presentation.

■ **Learn from feedback.** Whether you are an experienced presenter or a first-timer, there is always more to learn.

If you follow these 50 **secrets**, you will know everything you need to deliver a brilliant presentation. Your audience will remember your message and, just as importantly, they will remember you.

Whether you are an experienced presenter or a first-timer, you can make a positive impact on your audience and, just as importantly, enjoy doing so!

Prepare the basics

The success of your presentation will depend on preparation. This chapter explains the firm foundations you need to lay to make your presentation effective. It covers creative thinking, organizing your thoughts and undertaking research. This is the 'blank canvas' stage. You need to work through the ultimate aims of what you are planning to achieve. Think about who is in your audience and the best way to communicate with them.

1.1

Stand out from the crowd

First of all, take a step back from thinking about the content of your presentation and think about your own personality instead. Remember that your audience will be listening to and looking at a *presenter* as much as a presentation.

You don't want simply to deliver a series of data and facts. You want to put your soul into this presentation, and enjoy yourself in the process. The most interesting, memorable and effective presentations have the personality of their presenter stamped all over them. You want to put across your values and opinions, and your audience wants to hear them. Here are some tips to help you from the start to develop a really positive, creative view of yourself as an interesting presenter:

■ **Read something worthy.** Devour your favourite website. Read a quality newspaper e.g. *The Economist, Time, Newsweek.*
■ **Think. Don't just read.** Think through the big underlying issues. Schedule in time to relax your brain from concentrated action. Carry a pen and notebook with you, or digital equivalents. Jot down your thoughts and ideas – however odd they may be. They may be useful.

"Don't measure yourself by what you have accomplished, but by what you should have accomplished with your ability"

John Wooden, legendary basketball coach

■ **Really listen to people.** What they're saying… and not saying. Reflect on what you're learning. Talk with friends and colleagues. Discuss issues and ideas; express your latest thinking to gauge responses. Develop ideas you feel passionate about.

■ **Examine your values and principles**. What motivates you? Life is full of decisions. What spurs you on?

■ **Care for others.** Don't become so absorbed with yourself that you neglect people around you, in your community and in the wider world. Take a stand on world issues, and engage in some practical action.

■ **Stretch yourself.** What areas of life that are currently weak do you want to develop? Sketch them out and then begin to work on the next steps to fufil them.

■ **Don't take yourself too seriously.** Watch TV. Relax – and laugh at yourself.

■ **Cultivate your spiritual/emotional side.** Whether it's religion or poetry. We're not just thinking machines.

■ **Work on the physical side of your life.** Take control of your life. If you're out of condition, go to the gym regularly: if you want to lose weight, join a slimming class.

Cultivate a positive attitude about yourself as a great presenter.

1.2

Know your aims

It's vital to know why you are giving your presentation. It is important that you define the purpose of what you are presenting in one sentence. This will clarify what you should include – and what you can safely leave out. Having a concise, clearly expressed aim in front of you in all your preparation will help guide your thoughts.

Think why you have been asked to give a presentation. It may even be that a presentation is not the only way (and possibly not even the best way) of communicating a message.

See your presentation as one part of an aspect of the communications of your company or organization. Other ways of giving a message include email, the company intranet, a memo or report, posters, group discussion, one-to-one meetings, managers and bosses

one minute wonder In preparing a presentation, it can be very helpful to think of one typical person in the audience. Will he or she understand what you are saying and be persuaded by its message? Imagine you are talking to a personal friend.

"If you don't know where you are going, you will probably end up somewhere else"

Dr Laurence J. Peter and Raymond Hull, authors of The Peter Principle

who model certain behaviour to build trust. Ask the following questions about your presentation:

■ **Who is in the audience?** What are they like? What do they already know about the subject? You can then make sure that what you are saying is suitable for their level.

■ **What are the main messages?** Are you clear about the essential information and ideas you want to communicate?

■ **What do you want to achieve?** This is what you want people to do or think, understand or accept as a result of your presentation. Do you want colleagues to accept future sales forecasts? Or be persuaded to adopt a new product? How will you measure people's reactions to know whether you have fulfilled your aim?

■ **How are you going to make your presentation?** For example, how formal is it? Will you stand or sit? What visual aids will you use?

■ **How long will you speak for?** Will there be time for questions? What is the room like? How will the audience be seated?

■ **What's the big picture?** Where does your presentation fit into the overall picture of communications in your organization?

Work out exactly what you want to achieve with your presentation.

1.3

Know your audience

It's important that the focus of your presentation is your audience. You should do all you can to research your audience so that you can pitch at the right level. Here are eight things to think about.

1 How many people will be at your presentation? The way you give your presentation will vary greatly if the audience is five people, 20, or 200.

2 What does the audience already know about the subject? If you don't know, ask the organizer. Knowing this will enable you to decide whether to go over the basics and how much you will need to explain jargon.

case study Adam's failure was when he presented the keynote speech at a major conference. He knew that the company had paid a lot to secure the keynote slot, and he therefore assumed incorrectly that he had to do a hard sell. In reality, the audience was a group of distinguished analysts, and they were interested in

3 What are the attitudes or feelings of the audience likely to be towards the subject you are presenting – and to you?

4 What expectations does the audience have of you as the presenter?

5 Do members of the audience know one another? Do they have good relationships with one another?

6 Will members of the audience be present because they have to come to your presentation or because they want to be there?

7 Are there any hidden agendas or underlying tensions that you should be aware of?

8 Who are the decision makers in the audience? What are their opinions?

Find out as much as possible about your audience in advance.

industry trends. They reported later that the company still didn't understand the enterprise. What Adam should have done was simply inform them of the trends the company sees, and that would have built credibility and even positioned the company as market leader.

1.4

Consider how people learn

People learn in different ways. If you want to communicate effectively, you will vary the ways in which you present information. As a presenter, you should put yourself in the place of members of your audience. If you want to be sure of success, you should remember that people learn in different ways.

There are three main kinds of learning style:

1 **Visual learners.** Such people like to see information in pictures, diagrams, charts, tables and in writing.

case study Peter led a workshop on communication at which his wife was present. She pointed out to him during a coffee break that some members of the audience were losing interest and motivation. "Get them involved," she advised. Peter followed her

2 **Auditory learners.** Such people like to listen to information and then discuss it with others, listening to what others say, to help them learn.

3 **Kinaesthetic learners.** Such people like to be active and learn by doing.

In your preparation as presenter, you should be aware that people learn in different ways. Good presenters will use a multi-sensory approach to include different styles of learning so that every member of the audience will be able to take in the presentation effectively. This means that you should provide visual aids that illustrate and give headings to support your argument, provide opportunities for discussion and make room for expression through stories and role play.

In your preparation, explore different ways to make your presentation more effective.

advice and adjusted his method for the next section from presentation to role play: he divided the audience into three small groups which each took different parts. The result: a more highly-motivated audience and more effective learning.

1.5

Think creatively

Once you are clear about the aims of your presentation in your own mind, you are ready to move on to the next stage, which is to think creatively. Time spent thinking is not wasted: it will mean that your final presentation is clearly structured and easy to follow.

The best way to think creatively is to write about your thoughts in a pattern diagram sometimes called pattern notes, or Mind Map™. This is a creative diagram you draw that captures all the main aspects of your central thoughts as you see them. To do this, you should:

■ Take a blank sheet of A4 paper, arranging it in landscape format.
■ Write the central thought or theme (a word or a few words, not a whole sentence) of your presentation in the middle of the paper.
■ Write around that central word other keywords that relate to it.
■ Keep branching out, adding other points that come into your mind.

one minute wonder Acronyms can be a creative way of organizing thoughts and messages. Consider this **TOWER** acronym for the task ahead: **T**: thinking **O**: organizing your thoughts **W**: writing a first draft **E**: editing and **R**: revising the grammar.

"What is the hardest task in the world? To think"

Ralph Waldo Emerson, philosopher

■ If you get stuck at any point, answer the question words: who, why, where, what, when, how. These will stimulate your thinking.

■ At this stage, do not reject any thoughts. (Use an eraser sparingly to delete what you have written.)

■ As a next stage you can draw lines to show the links from your central thought to your key words and between individual key words.

■ You can colour in different key words to show which ones are related.

■ You can number the different key words in order of importance. Later on, as you deal with each aspect in your writing, you can put a line through each one.

As you draw a diagram of your own thoughts, you will probably see a clear structure with key messages beginning to emerge. (If this doesn't happen, leave the paper for a while and come back to it later.) Aim for between three and five key messages in your presentation. If you have more than five, you risk overloading your audience with too much information.

Time spent thinking creatively is not wasted.

1.6

Organize your thoughts

Spend time focusing on the key messages that you want to give in your presentation. Begin to arrange your key messages in a logical order. Having a clear structure helps your audience follow what you are saying more easily.

There are several different ways in which you can arrange the information that you want to present. You need to choose the best approach, depending on your audience. If you are unsure which way to adopt, discuss it with a colleague.

1 Move from facts to a conclusion. The audience listens to your presentation of the facts and they are led to a conclusion. If you follow this approach, the audience may have to think hard to follow your logic.

2 Start with a conclusion, then see how that conclusion is supported by certain facts and arguments. This is usually easier for audiences to follow than 1.

" Everyone gets so much information all day long that they lose their common sense **"** **Gertrude Stein, writer**

3 Persuade people to adopt a point of view, by giving different sides of an argument. Begin by stating your opinion, then give the arguments for and against that opinion and finally draw conclusions from what you have said.

4 Give a list of options. Begin by stating a particular situation and then present the various possible solutions, with their advantages and disadvantages. Finally, outline the next possible steps.

5 Explain a process. Begin by stating how many steps are involved in the process. Say how each different stage works, with its end result. Summarize often. Often, a diagram will help clarify the different stages.

6 Include clear signposts of the route of your presentation. For example, "To start with; I will describe two different kinds of problem; on the one hand…, on the other…".

Spend time focusing on your key messages.

1.7

Research carefully

Inject your presentation with supporting evidence that will reinforce your key messages. Use a range of sources to investigate your subject. You might not use all the information you collect, but you will have thought through different issues.

Sources of information include:

■ **Data and statistics.**
■ **The Internet.** E.g. Wikipedia or www.Credoreference.com
■ **Libraries.** In our digital age, it is easy to ignore the valuable hard-copy resources of libraries that have been built up over the years. Librarians themselves also have a wealth of knowledge at their fingertips and will be able to point you in the right direction. Reference sections of

case study I was once given just three hours' notice to give a 45-minute presentation, and that included breakfast and travelling to the venue! Fortunately, the subject was close to my heart. I'd kept notes on treatments of similar subjects and could find them

libraries are an obvious source of information, while some people find that even a children's book on a subject provides a useful overview.

If you give many presentations, then it can be useful to keep an ideas book, either physically or digitally, of interesting items that could help you. Such items could include:

- Newspaper cuttings
- Extracts from journals or magazines
- Illustrations that are particularly striking
- Titles of books
- Quotations from public figures or leaders in your field
- Witty anecdotes
- Extracts you come across in your general reading
- Insightful comments in a blog

In your preparation be willing to think outside the box. Explore different perceptions of a sensitive issue. Distinguish between facts and opinions. Question well-known arguments. Go beyond face value.

Inject strong supporting evidence into your presentation to reinforce your message.

easily. I used a colleague's outline and structure as a basis and added my own personal anecdotes and approach. The keys to success were mental prepararation and being able to access vital information quickly.

1.8

Look at your venue

We've all known times when a good presentation has been spoilt by poor attention to practical details, for example when the speaker arrives late or speaks for too long. Do your best to make sure that nothing can go wrong. When thinking about your presentation, consider the details of the venue.

You need to think about the practical details of where you are physically going to give your presentation.

■ **How will you reach the venue in good time?** If you don't know the location of where you are speaking, work out how you are going to get there. Check the location on a map or check the postcode for your

case study Sarah once led a two-day seminar in Chicago. She booked into the hotel the evening before the first day and in the morning rang for a taxi to take her to the venue of the seminar. The taxi turned up fine and the first day of the course went well. She thought the same would happen the second day but she hadn't reckoned with the

satellite-navigation system. Find out what the car-parking facilities are. If you are travelling by train, check the railway timetable and where necessary book a taxi to take you from the railway station to the venue. Time spent on these matters in advance helps you feel more in control and prepared for possible delays or other unforeseen eventualities.

■ Think through the arrangements at the venue. Who will meet you, where and at what time? Remember to allow sufficient time from arriving at the venue to when you are scheduled to begin your presentation, to allow time to freshen up.

■ Check the lighting of the room. If possible, give your presentation in a room that has natural light.

■ Consider the ventilation of the room If the air in the room is too hot and stuffy, your audience will become drowsy. On the other hand, you don't want people to become cold. Check how to operate any air-conditioning or heating systems.

Make sure your presentation is not spoilt by poor attention to the practicalities set by the venue.

weather. On the morning of the second day it was raining heavily and all the taxis were busy already. She eventually arrived very late for the seminar – even at the point when some of the delegates were wondering if she'd ever arrive at all. The lesson: now she always books a taxi the evening before a presentation.

1.9

Consider the seating and accessories

You need to think through the facilities that you will need for your presentation. In particular, the way in which your seating is arranged has an important effect on the success of your presentation.

What accessories will you need at your presentation? You will probably bring your own laptop; will a projector be provided? Check that the power supply is close to your electrical equipment or that an extension lead is available. Again, allow enough time to check that your laptop connects properly with the projector. Will you need a flipchart? Flipchart pens?

one minute wonder How powerful is your voice? If the room is large, will a microphone and amplification equipment be provided? You will need to make sure you know how the equipment works and practise using it if at all possible.

■ **Rows and horseshoes.** Think through the seating arrangements. If your audience is large (over 30) and the seating is formal with little interaction, then the layout of seating in rows may be best. If the audience is 20-30 and there is room, then an arrangement in a horseshoe (semi-circle) works well. This allows participants to work in pairs or to talk to one another a little. The disadvantage, however, is that it does not facilitate teamwork or group discussion.

■ **Cabaret seating.** If one of your aims is to develop teamwork, interaction and discussion among the participants, then seating around tables ('cabaret style') works well, with five or six seated at each table, allowing room for workbooks, water, pens, etc. A possible disadvantage is that some participants may only be able to see you as presenter or if they turn around from the table.

■ **Furniture for you.** Think whether you will speak from a lectern or table, or without any furniture at all.

■ **Drinking water.** Will water be provided for you or should you take a bottle and glass with you?

Whichever layout you choose, give clear instructions to the organizers in advance, but also allow time before your presentation to check that your instructions have been carried out.

The seating arrangement, equipment and accessories need to be planned in advance.

1.10

Plan your stages

When planning your presentation, think through as far as you can the practical details of each stage of what you plan to do. Some of these practicalities may be outside your control, but at least you will have thought of them. If you give presentations regularly, then it would be good to compile a check list of the various items.

1 Have the phone number of your contact. (Their phone number is probably more important than their email address.) Keep that phone number near you, or key it into your mobile so you can access it quickly if you are delayed.

case study Max tries to get to a venue early, well before the time the presentation is due to begin, especially if he is going into a company for the first time. Once, he arrived half an hour early and immediately began to notice who was talking to who... and who wasn't talking to anyone else. One person

2 Know the time of your presentation: when you are due to begin and end; whether questions will be asked and, if so, if it will be during your talk or at the end. If they come at the end, will you chair the Question and Answer session or will someone else?

3 Know who will introduce you – or will you be expected to introduce yourself?

4 Know whether you bring your own handouts. Make sure you make enough photocopies in advance. Think about when you will distribute them.

5 Take your own pens, papers, post-it notes for last-minute changes and if necessary enough paper and pens for your audience.

Time spent planning the order of your presentation helps you stay in control.

offered to make Max a coffee, and colleagues expressed surprise as that person had never offered to make them a coffee. This information was helpful to Max later in the presentation when he encouraged colleagues who didn't usually interact to start talking to each other and begin working as a team.

Work on
your words

The words you say are the single most important part of your presentation. You need to work hard at the verbal content, varying your style and choosing your words carefully to keep your message simple and clear. Here is practical advice on planning the beginning, middle and end of your speech, and working out a title for the presentation.

2.1

Keep your message simple

Start preparing your presentation, making sure that your material is not complicated and will not demand too much of your audience. The audience is more likely to take in your information and enjoy your presentation if you keep it simple.

■ **Identify your key messages.** Think about what is the overriding point of what you are trying to say and break that down into a few (three to five) key messages. If you include more, you risk overloading your presentation. Less is more.

> **case study** Emily's talks on English grammar were too long. It was as if she were trying to communicate everything she knew on the subject. Gradually, Emily learnt that less is more. Her audience weren't looking for a reference-book "give us all the 50 things you

■ **Use short sentences.** When we write normal English, our sentences tend to be longer than when we speak. Keep your sentences to 10 to 15 words each.

■ **Use active verbs.** In the sentence, "Caroline broke the window", the verb "broke" is active. It is performed by the person who is named: Caroline. This contrasts with the sentence, "The window was broken by Caroline", in which the verb "broken" is passive. The window has an action done to it. "By Caroline" is optional: in a passive sentence, you do not need to say who has done the action. Passive verbs are longer and sound more formal; active verbs are shorter and sound more natural. They are also easier to understand, partly because a person is named early in the sentence. Use fewer passive verbs and more active verbs.

■ **Use short words.** Try to use only words of one or two syllables. Listen to songs written by the Beatles, as an example: most of their lyrics consist of one- or two-syllable words. Try not to use formal words, but words that we use in ordinary speech.

Focus on the main point of what you're trying to say.

know" approach, but Emily's personal appreciation of a subject: her own point of view on it. As she selected material that was appropriate to the audience and worked at expressing herself more simply, she gained happier, more responsive audiences.

2.2

Watch your language

Make sure your presentation uses words that are clear and easily understood by your audience. It takes time to work hard at refining the words you use to express your key messages. Here are some tips to help you use clear English.

■ **Avoid jargon and clichés.** For example, try not to use phrases such as "going forward", "downsizing", "a level playing field". Ask yourself or discuss with a colleague face to face (not by email) what you actually mean. Be ruthless with yourself – it is very important that you express your ideas clearly and simply.

■ **Be specific.** Avoid general statements. Your presentation will have a greater impact if you discuss a particular example. If you are talking about diversity among a population, then quoting an actual example of an event that celebrates diversity will be more effective than simply giving a list of different groups.

■ **Be accurate.** Use language precisely. One colleague wrote "interfere" when what he meant was "intervene". "Interfere" has a negative critical tone, suggesting an action that is uninvited. "Intervene" is more positive and can suggest a welcome move or action.

one minute wonder Why use a longer, more formal word when a shorter word is just as good, if not better? Stop for a moment to consider these examples, and always choose the simplest words when preparing your presentations.

additional	extra
cognizant of	aware of
commence	begin, start
endeavour	try
in excess of	more than
utilize	use

■ **Use fewer abstract nouns and more verbs.** For example, change "conduct an investigation" to "investigate"; change "suffer a deterioration" to "deteriorate".

■ **Move from the familiar to unfamiliar.** Start sentences with information that is familiar to your audience. Then move on to new information. Doing this the other way round – starting with new information and then moving to information already known – is more difficult for an audience to take in.

Be ruthless with language to make sure you express yourself clearly.

2.3

Vary your style

Use different methods to deliver your message and keep your audience interested and responsive to what you want to communicate. Here are some tried and tested ways in which you can add variety to your presentation.

■ **Tell a story.** I've sat in boring talks in which people have fallen asleep. When the speaker said "Let me tell you a story," I have seen rows of heads suddenly lift up to listen to a picture painted in words.

case study In a speech in 2008 on Millennium Development Goals, Prime Minister Gordon Brown used a variety of methods to deliver a powerful message. He included a story about the life and death of one boy to spur the world into action, as follows: "In the museum in Rwanda, which commemorates the thousands killed as the world looked on and looked the other way, there is a picture of a young boy who was tortured to death, and the plaque reads – Name: David; Age: 10; Favourite

■ **Mention a contemporary event.** Read the morning's newspaper to be able to quote an up-to-date story or feature.

■ **Bring out a table, graph or other visual aid.** See 3.2 for more on this subject.

■ **Refer to a map.** This is useful to show the location of an unfamiliar area or country.

■ **Use illustrations.** You can communicate something complicated with a well-chosen image. On the television news, for example, a story is usually accompanied by a picture behind or alongside the newsreader. When I give a talk, I often try to summarize a key message of the talk in a picture. It could be a picture of cartoon characters, or people, flowers or mountains: these can help your audience visualize what you are trying to express. Use your own digital pictures or non-copyright material from the Internet.

Think how you could express your key messages more creatively.

Sport: Football; Enjoyed: Making people laugh; Dream: Becoming a doctor; Last words: 'the United Nations will come for us' – But we never did. Even as he died, that child believed the best of us. In reality, our promises meant to him nothing at all. Today, facing famine, we promised we, the United Nations of the world, will come to help, but the hungry are dying while we wait. Facing poverty, we promise that we will come to help, but the poor are dying while we wait."

2.4

Choose your words carefully

Here are some further elements you might want to include in a creative, memorable speech.

■ **A quotation.** Consider this one for example: "A word aptly spoken is like apples of gold in settings of silver." (The Bible, Proverbs 25:11)

■ **An allusion.** This is where you make a casual reference to something else that the audience should understand and make a connection with the subject. For example, "painting the Forth Bridge" should be understood by a British audience as a reference to undertaking an apparently

case study Louis led a presentation on the power of words. He broke the ice at the beginning of his talk by recalling an anecdote by the late Clement Freud, the British cookery expert, MP and broadcaster. Freud would send cards to his constituents at significant events in their lives, such as weddings or bereavements. What he had not prepared for, however, was the response this would lead to. Members of the public

never-ending task. Or if you mentioned someone as "having their 15 minutes of fame", you are alluding to pop artist Andy Warhol's comment about the media. Obviously, you need to be confident that your audience will be culturally receptive to any allusion you make.

■ **A dictionary definition.** To say, for example, that the *Collins English Dictionary* defines a presentation as "a verbal report presented with illustrative material, such as slides, graphs, etc" makes you sound more authoritative.

■ **A question.** Asking questions makes people think. A rhetorical question is one given as a statement rather than one that is expected to be answered. "Do you think questions work?"

■ **Speaking in threes.** This increases the impact of your message, adds rhythm to your talk and makes you sound more authoritative. Using alliteration for the different parts of your talk, for example three words beginning with R.

Words are a powerful tool: choose them with care.

would come up to him in the street, expecting him to know them personally, which of course he didn't. For a while he didn't know how to respond – whether happily if the news was good or with proper respect if the news was bad. Later he worked out a response, which covered every eventuality: "It was the least I could do." This anecdote went down very well with Louis's audience and established a good rapport.

2.5

Make clear notes

Only the most experienced speakers use no notes. The rest of us need something, especially because it's a common problem to feel nervous and forget what you were about to say. Having some form of text in front of you is reassuring. The main choice is whether to write out your full speech or simply refer to notes.

Points about writing out the text in full:

■ Allows you to think through the exact emphasis you want to place in your presentation.

■ Should be used as a basis, or a 'backstop' if you forget your words in your actual delivery or the direction in which you are going.

■ Works well if you increase the font size of the script after typing it and also if you highlight the key phrases and points that you want to make.

■ Means you may have several A4 pages to turn over in the course of the speech. This may work if you have a lectern but could be distracting if you have to hold the sheets of paper.

"When something can be read without effort, great effort has gone into its writing"

Enrique Jardiel Poncela, Spanish writer

Points about writing notes:

■ Many speakers write notes, rather than a full text. Experienced speakers often say that to begin with they wrote out their presentations in full but after some time and increased confidence, they have come to write in note form.

■ If you write your presentation in notes, you could write on 10 cm x 15 cm cards, with headings and subheadings, which act as memory joggers.

■ Speaking from notes allows you to maintain good eye contact with the audience, so you can gauge their response. If they are not following you, then you have the flexibility to repeat your point in different words or using a different approach.

Write down your entire presentation or, at the very least, some notes.

2.6

Choose a compelling title

A good title will attract an audience; it will invite interest. It should reflect the content of your presentation, be memorable and not too long or obscure.

You may have to work out your title even before you have written a presentation, so that the event can be publicized. As you think creatively, research and organize your material, a title may emerge (if you've not already been given one). Ideally, the title should be catchy and snappy. Here are some pointers.

1 What level is it pitched at? If basic: *An Introduction to... Essential... An Overview of...* If intermediate: *Better... Developing your skills in...* If advanced, then: *Advanced... Professional...*

2 Be intriguing: *Secrets of...* What drew you to a series of books labelled *Business Secrets*?

3 Do you want to focus on the process you are talking about or on the end result? *How to ... Successful...*

4 What do you want your audience to get out of your presentation? *Effective…*

5 How long do members of your audience need to take to obtain results from your advice: *…in Five Days …in a Day … in an Hour.*

6 Who is your presentation aimed at: *…for Managers …for Students.*

7 What results does your audience want to achieve: *…with Confidence.*

8 Focus on a key part of your presentation. For example, a presentation on the challenges that older people face in using technology could have the title: *Computers: Friend or Foe?*

It's best to be straightforward in your title, making sure that it is appropriate to the content. Alliteration can work (I had *Loose Language can Lose Business* and *Whizzing up your Website*) or you can take an idiomatic phrase, *Put It in Writing*, or a question, pun, quotation or allusion, e.g. *Medication: a Bitter Pill to Swallow?* or *Security: Who will Guard the Guards?*

Your title should be catchy and snappy.

2.7

Plan your beginning

First impressions are vital. We all know that human beings reach very quick conclusions about each other. See this as an opportunity, not as a threat. Take the chance to tell the audience what your presentation is going to be about. After all, the first few minutes of the presentation are the only time when you can guarantee everyone is paying you their full attention.

Your introduction needs to address five different topics. Conveniently, they spell out the word **INTRO**.

■ **I = Interest.** Raise interest in yourself and your topic. Give some background to yourself. Explain your experience and credentials briefly. Why is your topic relevant? Why is it particularly relevant now? And why are you qualified to talk about it? An example of a recent news story or YouTube video can often make a good opener.

■ **N = Need.** Explain why your audience needs to listen to your presentation. Will it make their life easier? Will it make them richer? A clear, concise example of an organization or person you previously have helped can be useful here.

one minute wonder It's normally difficult to find someone prepared to listen to your whole presentation in advance. But most people will be happy to listen to your introduction. Find a colleague who is in your target audience, see what their response to your introduction is, and act on their advice.

■ **T = Timing.** Tell your audience how long you will speak for. This is very helpful to prepare your audience mentally, particularly if they are worried they might miss lunch or a flight. Make sure you stick to your promised timing.

■ **R = Response.** Tell your audience how and when they can participate. Should they interrupt you while you speak? Will there be time for questions at the end?

■ **O = Objective.** This is when you tell your audience what the purpose and scope of the presentation are. Don't be afraid of repeating yourself.

These steps are useful for the audience because it will condition them for what to expect. But they are also useful for the speaker. They will focus your mind, and you'll find that by the time you get them out of the way you will be right into the meat of your presentation.

The introduction is your opportunity to let the audience know what to expect.

2.8

Work out the middle

The middle of a presentation is like the filling in a sandwich. It is the key part of what you are saying. Unfortunately, it is also the point at which your your audience's attention may start to wander.

The audience will have concentrated on your beginning and will prick up their ears when you introduce your conclusion with, "Finally…" (see 2.9). You must do all you can to maintain your audience's attention in the central part of your presentation.

1 Vary the style of what you are saying (see 2.3). Ask challenging questions. Express your message in a story. Quote an up-to-date event. Work hard at finding fresh ways to communicate your message.

2 Spread out your key points throughout your presentation. Don't give everything in your first key point. That may be the most important message you are trying to communicate – the one thing you want your audience to take away – but you need also to have other key points to support your argument.

3 Make sure your presentation is arranged logically, that its points are ordered in such a way that one follows on naturally from another. If the logic isn't clear to you, it will not be clear to your audience. Subdivide major points into clear sub-points.

4 Make sure that your evidence, e.g. facts and figures, clearly supports your argument and is consistent with its conclusions. If this is not so, attentive listeners will point out, "You said earlier in your talk that sales would rise by 5%, yet later you hinted that it might be 15%. Which is correct?"

5 Vary the ways in which you present your information. If the subject is appropriate, involve your audience in role play. Ask the audience to break into small groups to discuss a question. If you do this, be clear about what you want them to talk about, how much time you are giving them and whether they will feed back some of their responses to the whole group.

6 Take an unscheduled break. If the members of the audience don't know one another, say, "Let's take a break for a couple of minutes. Why don't you stand up and stretch you legs. If you don't know the people sitting round you, why not introduce yourself to them?" (Remember to allow for the fact that a couple of minutes may well turn into five.)

Do all you can to maintain your audience's attention in the central part of your talk.

2.9

End on a high

The final part of your presentation is very important. Your conclusion may well be the part that remains with your audience for a long time afterwards. You therefore need to work hard to make sure it gives the message you want it to.

When you are preparing your presentation, you may well begin to lose some of your interest and motivation as you come near to preparing your conclusion. The temptation is to give up, do nothing and see what happens. If you do that, however, you are not giving the proper careful attention to your ending that it deserves, nor full credit to the hard work you have put in up to this point.

one minute wonder Think about what response you want from members of your audience. What are the next steps you want them to take after you've delivered your presentation? Be practical.

1 Begin with a signal that you are now coming to the end of your presentation. For example, say, "Finally let's draw all these thoughts together."

2 Your conclusion should bring together all the key messages of your presentation up to that point. Restate your earlier key messages. Don't include any significantly new material in your conclusion.

3 Emphasize the one key message that you have tried to communicate in your presentation.

4 Include a clear statement of what response you would like members of your audience to make… what the next steps are that you want them to take. Say, "The one thing I'd like you to take away from today is…" Be practical. For example, say, "As the next step, you could agree to implement the report's findings."

5 End with a signal that you have now finished. For example, say, "Thank you for your attention. I'd now be very happy to answer your questions."

Think of a great ending to do justice to all the hard work you have put in.

Plan for props and other people

Most presenters want to avoid standing alone in a room and talking without a single prop. Visual and audio aids will support your presentation and give it impact. This chapter explores a variety of tools from traditional aids such as handouts and flipcharts to PowerPoint. It also covers video conferencing and presenting with other people in a team.

3.1

Make good use of handouts

Handing out printed notes to members of an audience is a popular prop for presenters. I personally prefer to distribute handouts early on so that the audience can see the overall messages that I am trying to communicate. Here are some top tips about using handouts effectively.

1 Make sure that the text does not fill the whole page. Leave space for members of your audience to write their own notes.

2 Make the font larger than you would use in a letter, so the audience can read it easily and listen to you at the same time.

case study In one of Joe's early talks, he made the mistake of providing a handout that was almost the complete text of what he said. It took up several pages, and his delivery of the presentation consisted mainly of reading the handout aloud,

3 It is better to cut parts out of your text than try to squeeze too much onto a handout. (If you don't know what to cut, take a break and come back to the text later; usually you will then be able to see what can be removed.)

4 Decide when to distribute your handouts. Distributing them early has the advantage that your audience can follow what you are saying and add their own notes. The disadvantage is that they may read the notes instead of listening to you. If you decide to distribute them later, tell your audience at the beginning that is what you are going to do.

5 Remember that distributing paper will actually take up part of your time; therefore consider putting them out on tables or chairs before your presentation.

6 Keep a copy of the handout of your presentation with you to refer to alongside your full notes or text.

7 Take advantage of technology: for example, print out slides of your PowerPoint on Outline View, or make your handout notes available later by email.

Use handouts to reinforce your key messages.

occasionally adding a few other comments. After the presentation, a helpful friend pointed out to him, "Why did we need to come and listen to your talk when we could have read it all from your paper?" He now summarizes the talk in his handout.

3.2

Present tables and charts skilfully

If you need to communicate anything relating to numbers, then you will probably want to show some kind of table, graph, chart or diagram. These can be very effective tools in presentations.

These styles of chart are popular in presentations:

■ **Bar chart.** Has bars of equal width but with different heights in proportion to the values they stand for. Useful for comparing quantities over time.

■ **Pie chart.** A circle divided into slices of differing sizes. Useful for comparing data in proportion to a whole, but can be difficult for the eye to take in quickly. Keep to a maximum of five slices.

■ **Gantt chart.** Type of bar chart that illustrates the duration of certain tasks over time. Useful for planning and scheduling.

■ **Flow chart.** A line graph showing the relationship between two kinds of information (along the vertical and horizontal axes) and how they vary depending on each other. Often used to illustrate a series of steps, the stages of a process, or changes or trends over time.

Whatever style of table, graph, chart or diagram you choose, bear in mind these points:

1 Don't include too much information; show only the key data. Keep your presentation clear, simple and uncluttered.

2 Use colour to make the graphs, tables and charts instantly more appealing and memorable. Also use clear titles, with concise sub-headings and labels. Make sure that the numbers are printed large enough to be legible.

3 Bear in mind that people visually take in figures presented in columns more easily than those presented in rows. For example if you are comparing data, put the numbers in adjacent columns, not rows.

4 Also for the sake of clarity, round numbers up or down consistently, e.g. not 9.1637 and 8.43, but 9.2 and 8.4.

5 Finally, double check your numbers. If someone spots that your percentages add up to 95% ... or 105%, not only will you be embarrassed but also you might be forced on the spot to recalculate and explain how you came to make the error.

Illustrate numbers in the simplest way possible, and make sure they add up.

3.3

Freedom is a flipchart

Flipcharts may be relatively low-tech but they are a flexible and versatile tool. They work best in an informal meeting with up to 50 participants. You can write and draw things on the pages in advance and/or during the presentation itself. You don't have to show or do things in a set order, so you have the freedom to respond to your audience as you go.

Flipcharts are useful for recording creative ideas and suggestions and involving your audience more so than is possible when doing a PowerPoint presentation. They are also helpful in teaching, highlighting and explaining particular difficulties that members of your audi-

case study When Juanita begins one of her courses on Report Writing, she often begins by asking delegates a simple question: "What makes a good report?" She then writes down on a flipchart the thoughts and ideas they suggest. At the end of that

ence might have. As a presenter, you can gradually reveal information, rather than giving it all at the same time. If you are planning to write on a flipchart during the actual presentation, bear in mind these tips:

1 Write clearly and neatly. You could also write beforehand in pencil on the flipchart any hard words that you find difficult to spell. The audience will not be able to see the pencil marks.

2 Talk only when you are not writing on the flipchart. If you talk while writing, your back will be to the audience so there will be no eye contact and your voice will be less clearly heard.

3 Make sure there are enough unused sheets of paper on the flipchart for you to complete your presentation.

4 Take your own pens (which you know will work). Use black and blue colours so that the text stands out and occasionally others, e.g. red or green.

Using a flipchart gives you flexibility on the order of your presentation.

part of the session, she tears off the sheet of paper from the easel and sticks it on the wall as a reminder of the points covered. Juanita finds the flipchart is a flexible way of easily recording participants' opinions and so increasing their involvement.

3.4

Master the technology

Using a laptop and projector, or other video or audio system adds instant dynamism to a presentation. As with anything relating to technology, though, there are possibilities of equipment blips and failure. Make sure that the technological aid genuinely adds content to your presentation and is not just there for show.

■ **Using PowerPoint.** This piece of software has been used by millions of people around the world to present slideshows of text and images in presentations. It has the benefits of enabling you to change your presentation at the last minute, and easily incorporate screenshots and video and imagery. However, using PowerPoint can be rather a cliché these days, especially if you fall into certain traps with using it. See 3.5 to avoid committing the Seven Deadly PowerPoint Sins.

■ **Using videos.** Be clear about your exact aims in using video. A brief two-minute clip from YouTube will probably be more successful than a rambling 12-minute video, which may turn an audience off. If you do need to show a video, make sure you test the specific video on the

> **"**Any sufficiently advanced technology is indistinguishable from magic**"** **Arthur C. Clarke, science fiction author**

specific presentation machine and projector. This is because some laptops like to show the video only on the laptop screen, even if the slides show up fine on the projector.

■ **Using audio.** Make sure your audio volume is correct before you start. Laptop speakers can be unreliable, and you don't want to frustrate your audience while you fiddle with the controls. If the volume is low, you'll lose the intro words/sounds. If the volume is too loud, you'll shock your audience and it will take some time to regain their attention.

■ **Using material from the Internet.** Online libraries of clip art (ready-made images that can be used to illustrate a wide range of subjects) are among the most visited content sites on the Internet. If you can't find what you want from the clip art libraries, you could try a general image search on standard search engines. However, check the copyright status of images before using them, because some sources do not allow any form of reproduction unless there is a credit or a fee is paid.

■ **Using fonts.** If you have to use a different computer in your presentation from the one on which you created the original text, bear in mind that the fonts are likely to look different. Ideally, load the same fonts onto the other machine in advance, but check that you are allowed to copy any licensed fonts.

Use technological props with caution.

3.5

Don't let PowerPoint ruin your presentation

In the 1990s, it was cutting edge to use Microsoft's PowerPoint software in presentations. Now, you need a good reason to do so – flipcharts are cool again. If PowerPoint isn't adding anything to your presentation, then don't use it.

If you are using PowerPoint, then mind these Seven Deadly PowerPoint Sins:

1 Don't accidentally make it illegible. Stick to large fonts (no more than six lines per page) and clearly distinguished colours (red on grey, yellow on blue, black on white).

2 Don't just write up what you are saying. People will read it instead of listening to you. Use the slides to illustrate your point but not to make your point.

3 Don't put too much text on the page. Keep your points simple. Avoid sub-points if possible.

one minute wonder Think back to the last PowerPoint presentation you saw (or gave). Were any of the Seven Deadly PowerPoint Sins committed? What could be done differently next time?

4 Don't use distracting effects like fancy page-turn animations. The presentation is not about your PowerPoint skills, and your audience has probably seen all the effects before.

5 Don't leave everything to the last minute. Make sure you have time to arrive early and ensure that the PowerPoint works in its setting and, just as importantly, you know how to use it.

6 Don't talk to the screen. Make sure your eye contact is with the audience, not with the screen, and not with the remote control.

7 Don't be totally reliant on PowerPoint. Make sure you have a backup plan in the event that the technology fails.

Make sure you don't fall into the most common traps when using PowerPoint.

3.6

Try video conferencing

Setting up a video conference allows participants at two or more different locations to see one another and talk face to face in a 'virtual' space. This can save on the time and costs of travel, but it creates extra challenges in planning and delivering a presentation.

When setting up a presentation via live video feed, use this checklist:

■ Confirm the time of the meeting, especially if this involves different world time zones.

■ Schedule the meeting in a room with a good appearance and acoustics.

one minute wonder If you are going to be video conferencing from a webcam in your own home, make sure you have enough bandwidth to stream the live video, and that you have opened the correct port in your firewall. You will need to dress for a business meeting, even if no-one is in the room with you, and banish children and pets.

■ Clear the room of any distracting objects, e.g. bags, that could restrict the view or distract participants in other locations. Make sure all mobile phones are switched off.

■ Make sure all equipment – camera, projector, screen, microphones, loudspeakers, and Internet connections are all working properly. Don't put your laptop next to the microphone as the fan will generate noise and disrupt the meeting.

■ Work out a clear agenda for your meeting in advance, noting who will do what, and circulating that to all participants in advance. Clarify who will chair the meeting, introduce participants, etc. Work out in advance how graphics will be sent or shared.

■ Put name cards clearly in front of individuals. This helps you and everyone else involved.

■ Make sure a translator is available if you are video conferencing with people whose first language is different to your own. Heavy accents can make verbal communication difficult.

■ Minimize possible interruptions. Think through what might happen (e.g. fire-alarm tests?) to minimize possible interruptions.

■ Make sure participants face the camera while talking. Sometimes people are so nervous that they forget to do this.

■ Remember there may be a slight time delay that can lead to people trying to talk at the same time. When you are delivering the presentation, ask everyone to go on 'mute'.

Video conferencing saves on the time and expense of travel, but needs careful planning.

3.7

Work with a team

There are many advantages in working as a team and making a joint presentation, but only if everyone works well and unselfishly together and they know what is expected of them.

If you are working as part of a team, allow extra time in advance to discuss how you are going to work together. You will need to decide:

■ **Who will speak and on what different aspect of a subject?** In more significant presentations, appoint colleagues to fulfil particular roles, e.g. manager (someone with good people skills), administrator and technical expert.

■ **In what order should colleagues speak?** Here, think about not only the order of the actual content but also the need for variety in

case study Hassan was asked to lead a three-hour presentation on the benefits of new IT equipment. He quickly realized that he would need to involve people with technical skills to set up the equipment itself in the training room, and people to demonstrate different pieces of software, as well as dealing with queries from participants who were unfamiliar

"There is no 'I' in team-work" Anonymous

delivery. For example, follow someone who is speaking without any visual aids with a colleague who has visual diagrams or charts. Or make sure someone who is very serious in their approach is followed by someone whose tone is lighter.

■ **Who will introduce and close the group presentation?** And how you will deal with handovers from one colleague to another.
■ **Who will respond to questions from the audience?**
■ **When will you rehearse?** Some kind of rehearsal is essential to show up any gaps, repetitions or difficulties with handovers.

During the actual presentation it is important that team members who are not speaking look with interest and enthusiasm at their colleague who is speaking. It is also important that colleagues should respect what has been decided in advance and should not move into the territory already allocated to one of their colleagues.

Make sure you thoroughly plan and rehearse everything with your team.

with the new technology. He chose his team carefully and they developed their own parts of the presentation individually, then rehearsed twice together in the actual room. Once he knew what each of the team was going to cover, Hassan practised introducing them and also planned for chairing a question and answer session at the end.

Prepare your rmind

So you're prepared ... or at least you think you are. You've written the text, you've worked on some good ideas for visual aids, and you know what you're going to say. However, you lack confidence. This chapter will help calm your nerves and bring back your energy and enthusiasm.

4.1

Give yourself a pep talk

Be natural and be confident in your own personality. You have a unique background with all the experiences that have brought you to where you are now. Some will have been good: be happy in them. Some will have been bad: try to learn lessons from them.

There is an element of performance in giving a presentation. You are trying to impress your audience. The secret is to learn to be confident – and you can only be confident if you know what you're going to say and how you're going to express it.

If you work hard at preparing your presentation, you will develop a natural energy, enthusiasm and passion for it. If you aren't passionate about the subject, you can't expect your audience to be. If you deal with

case study A few years ago John's daughter got married. A video was taken at the reception and recorded his speech. John can still recall the shock at seeing himself – and the way in which he stood and spoke. At first he was critical of himself and only registered the parts

possible difficulties or problems as part of your preparation, you will find that sincerity and excitement will develop naturally as you speak.

Don't try to be like someone else when you are giving your presentation. It is OK to be inspired and helped by others, but do not follow others' actions or gestures. Your audience will soon realize that you are pretending to be something (or someone) you are not.

Here are some methods that will help you be more at ease with yourself:

■ **Record your voice.** Try recording parts of your speech while you practise. You will get used to the sound of your own voice when you play back, as well as noticing elements such as timing.
■ **Watch yourself on video.** Dig out old videos of yourself, especially any of you making a speech or performing in something. If at all possible, video yourself giving your presentation to an audience of family and friends. This will reveal how an audience gives you their attention. It may also show up odd personal habits such as fiddling with your hair.
■ **Practise assertiveness.** If you are naturally a quiet or shy person, you will need to learn to be more assertive. Read section 6 on body language. Practise standing tall and saying what you really feel. If you are already bold and self-confident, then this will come naturally to you.

You can do this.

of his speech that hadn't worked so well, but after watching the video several times over, he got used to the way he looked and sounded, and noticed that he had raised more smiles and laughs in his audience than he had realized at the time.

4.2

Build up your confidence

You can learn to be confident even if you feel the opposite right now. People often dwell too much on where things have gone wrong in the past. Don't become preoccupied with your bad experiences of presentations, whether your own or someone else's; instead learn from them.

■ **Think about why you have been asked to give the presentation.**
Probably it's because you know the subject well or because of your great experience. If others have confidence that you can do a good job, then that is a good start in itself.

case study I've become confident in speaking at presentations. But there is one area in my life that I am not confident in; my swimming ability. I worry if, for example, I am due to go on a boat trip on rough water. When I take seminars, I often share my lack of confi-

■ **Remember there is an element of performing.** Although you can still be yourself, there will be times when you don't feel confident. Be firm with yourself to go beyond your feelings of self-doubt.

■ **Prepare thoroughly.** Go back over chapters 1 and 2 of this book. Consider not only what the audience will be thinking… but also what they will be feeling. A secret of successful presentations is that you have thought through the issues you're likely to come across. Practise your presentation (see 4.4).

■ **Work on your one key message.** Make sure you can sum up the most important part of your message briefly. Then if all the technology fails, you can still communicate the key point effectively.

■ **Be confident in the style you adopt for presenting.** I don't feel comfortable talking all the time when I am presenting; I like to ask questions to see whether my audience are in tune with what I am saying.

■ **Be positive; don't talk down to your audience.** Keep them in mind; adjust what you are saying to them.

■ **Remember the additional aspects of your presentation.** The stories, the facts, the quotations that will add colour to your key message. Think about which spoke most clearly to you… and that will be the one that comes across with most enthusiasm and passion.

If others have confidence in you, then have some confidence in yourself!

dence (and low motivation) in this area, as it shows my participants that I understand what it's like to have serious doubts about something. Because I have confided in them a weakness, they don't feel so bad about any personal insecurities they feel.

4.3

Manage your nerves

Many speakers become nervous before a presentation. Symptoms of nervousness include your breathing becoming shallow, your mouth drying up, having a feeling of nausea and your body becoming tense. The trick is to learn to work through the anxiety. You can overcome your nervousness by:

■ **Focusing on something apart from yourself.** Think about your audience. They probably won't detect your nervousness. Remember you probably know more than they do. Most of them want you to succeed and are on your side. Go through the key points of your message again in your mind.

■ **Breathing deeply.** I've found this the most helpful practical technique when I'm becoming tense. Taking long deep breaths in and out will naturally relax your body.

case study Recently Jia led a course on the character of a person who helped others. She was nervous before it started as it was with a group of people she didn't know well. Fortunately, Jia had prepared well and she also had in mind a word beginning with

"There are two types of speakers, those that are nervous and those that are liars" Mark Twain, author

■ **Drinking water.** Just take tiny sips if you are so tense you cannot swallow properly. Don't drink alcohol.

■ **Trying to appear confident.** You have done your preparation. You have worked hard at your presentation. You have every right to see that all your hard work should make you look, if not actually be, confident.

■ **Being practical.** Write out your beginning and end and memorize the key points. Arrive early. Practise your presentation in advance. Time how long your presentation lasts.

■ **Controlling your thoughts.** You've worked hard on your presentation; now work on your imagination. Visualize yourself going on the stage, speaking confidently, and your audience smiling and receiving your presentation warmly. This will challenge negative thoughts.

■ **Smiling a lot.** Reminding yourself of a funny joke or story may steady your nerves.

You can overcome nervousness with these methods.

each of the first five letters of the alphabet: **A** attentive; **B** brave; **C** caring; **D** disciplined; **E** encouraging. Repeating these in her mind allowed Jia to concentrate on the delivery, rather than focusing on her nervousness.

4.4

Practise your presentation

One of the best ways to increase your self-confidence is by rehearsing. The more you practise, the deeper the message is reinforced in your mind. When it comes to actually giving your presentation, you will be able to maintain good eye contact with your audience and appear confident and relaxed.

Ways to practise:

1 **Speak out loud.** Don't think that saying the words in your head is enough. You may well find you have missed out a step in your argument and that you need to revise certain parts. I put an X by the side of my notes when rehearsing and a brief comment about what needs revising, which I go back to after I have finished rehearsing.

2 **Ask colleagues or friends for their opinion.** For example, on any parts of your presentation that you are not sure about. "Does this sound OK?" "Can I say this?" Ask for their honest thoughts and be brave enough to follow them.

"All the real work is done in the rehearsal period"

Donald Pleasance, English actor

3 **Time yourself.** One of the benefits of rehearsing is that it gives you an estimate of how long your presentation is likely to last. You can even write down on your notes where you should be by a certain time, e.g. Here by 11 o'clock.

4 **Practise with your visual aids.** Don't just practise with your script – do it also with your PowerPoint or other visual aids. Again, you will see what is effective and what doesn't work so well. Give yourself time to make any necessary adjustments.

5 **Speak into a microphone.** This is particularly important if you are going to be using a hand-held microphone, because holding one will mean that you cannot use both hands for gestures. If you don't have access to a real microphone when practising, use your mobile phone or a thick flip-chart pen instead.

6 **Work out your pacing.** For example, when to pause... and when to emphasize the key messages. When rehearsing presentations, I often underline or highlight the key phrases in colour; the visual impression reinforces them more deeply in my mind.

The more you practise, the deeper the message is reinforced in you.

4.5

Be enthusiastic

We've all sat through boring talks. The material may have been clear and logically structured, but the speaker was so half-hearted that it made no impact. At the other end of the scale, enthusiasm is also infectious. If you are excited about the subject, then your lively interest will spread to your audience.

Examine your passion for the subject. Have you become excited by your presentation? Have you considered your subject from every angle so much that it really lives inside you as something vital? Do you feel compelled to share it with others? Do you have a burning conviction within yourself that the approach you are advocating is clearly the best way forward? Is your enthusiasm greater than any inner reserve that might hold you back?

case study When Ashok first started giving talks, he would write the word 'smile' on the top right-hand corner of each sheet of paper. That reminded him to pause and look enthusiastic and

■ **Give your body and soul.** Giving a good presentation is more than ticking all the right boxes; it's about being an enthusiastic communicator: it's about varying the pitch of your voice, showing you are excited by your subject in your body language, expressing your emotions by smiling, being lively in your movement.

■ **Push the personal approach.** Believe in yourself and the topic you are presenting. Work at your presentation; research and know it so thoroughly that you become passionate about it. Make your presentation your own. Don't simply repeat what you have been told. Some of the material may be standard, but give your presentation your own distinctive approach. Inject your own personal ideas and text into it.

■ **Focus on your audience.** The presentation is not primarily about you and your performance; it's about moving your audience on in their understanding and response. While you're giving your presentation, be ready to adapt your style to make sure that you communicate as effectively as possible. Involve your audience where possible, through using different methods, e.g., role play or buzz groups (see 5.2).

■ **Begin and end well.** Be crisp and provocative in your introduction. End strongly. If you want your audience to respond in a certain way, make sure it's clear what the next steps are.

Make sure your enthusiasm spreads to your audience.

to show some passion in his presentation. Sometimes, members of the audience have commented that they have appreciated his smile and clear passion for his subject.

Interact with your audience

An audience will learn well when it feels comfortable with the presenter. This chapter explores strategies on how to build and keep a good relationship with your audience. Good listening skills are vital, and humour plays an important role. Another point is not to overload the audience by cramming in too much information.

5.1

Break the ice

It's often the case that participants in a presentation don't know each other and need to be introduced. Here are some suggestions to help 'break the ice' in a creative way that helps everyone to relax.

1 The traditional introduction phase is to ask each person to speak in turn: "Say your name, job role and what you are hoping you will get out of the presentation." As an alternative, ask them to introduce the person on their right. This will mean that they will have to spend a few minutes finding out the other person's name, job, working background, hobbies or interests.

2 Or ask them the question "What kind of car do you see yourself as? Why?" as well as their name, job role etc.

case study One of the most successful ice-breakers Tim experienced was at the beginning of a day conference in London. Because of major public-transport difficulties, many participants arrived late and were already tense and stressed before the day's sessions began. The conference organizer was

one minute wonder Get to your presentation early so that you can greet the first participants to arrive. Smile and reach out your hand to shake theirs, introducing yourself while looking directly at them. "Good morning, my name is Martin. I'm leading the presentation today."

3 Draw a personal logo that you think reflects your own personality or interests. Ask them to do the same.

4 Write the names from famous partnerships (e.g. Adam and Eve, Laurel and Hardy) on sticky labels. Stick one name on the back of each participant. Explain that the purpose is to find their partner in the room: they can ask such questions as, "Am I a person in a novel?" but can only answer with "Yes" or "No".

Find ways to help people relax and get to know each other before you give the main part of the presentation.

aware of this and spent the first 15 minutes reading out birthday cards – from the ordinary to the remarkable. Most were very funny and it soon relaxed members of the audience. All the tension disappeared quickly. After this, the group was ready to listen to the speaker's presentation.

5.2

Keep the momentum going

The average length of time that someone can focus on solid spoken input is 20 minutes. You need to involve your participants to maintain their attention, interest and motivation in presentations that are going to last longer than this.

This is especially important for meetings that take place after lunch when sessions should be particularly dynamic in order to stop participants' attention from drifting. In the seminars that I lead, I work on the principle that what participants learn most effectively is what they themselves actually say and do, not what I say to them. Here are some ways in which you can keep the momentum going.

case study Justine leads presentations about the use of Mind Maps™ (diagrams of ideas). She divides the presentation into three stages. In the first stage she shows examples of Mind Maps. In the second stage she ask participants to write a Mind Map of some-thing that is part of their life not related to their work. Typical examples are: planning a holiday or planning

■ **Ask questions.** Rather than give your audience the answers, open up a subject by asking an open-ended question. Write down the responses on a flipchart, acknowledging each answer with a "good" or "well done". At the end, weigh up the relative importance of the answers and add your own thoughts on important points missed.

■ **Play games.** Get teams to compete against one another to complete a task in the best and fastest way.

■ **Ask your audience if they've understood.** "Does this make sense?" If it doesn't, go back over your material more slowly and if necessary in a slightly different form.

■ **Form buzz groups.** Divide up the group into smaller groups of three to six people and give each a short assignment; ask them to appoint someone to report back to the larger group.

■ **Ask colleagues to work in pairs.** Ask them to discuss a particular point or give them tasks to complete. I often ask participants to discuss or work in pairs – one person's lack of confidence or knowledge is often balanced out by their colleague's greater confidence or knowledge.

■ **Engage in role play.** Act out a scenario, which will make people think and work through the issues for themselves.

What participants learn most is what they themselves actually say and do.

a marriage. She usually asks at least one of the participants to talk through what they have written. For the third stage, she asks participants to devise a Mind Map of something relating to their work. Because of their active involvement in the earlier two stages, this final task comes relatively easily to them.

5.3

Introduce some humour

Humour relaxes your audience and is an effective way of communicating your message and helping your audience remember it. Your presentation will be an enjoyable experience if you incorporate a little humour, but don't go over the top.

Gentle humour, especially when it is timed right and fits in with the situation and is part of your character, relaxes the audience. Beware of too much humour, though. Your main task is to give a presentation, not to be funny all the time. Beware of telling actual jokes; they won't work if they are at the expense of people of a different ethnicity, sex or age. You don't want to offend or alienate parts of your audience. Examples of gentle humour that works:

1 **Personal stories.** From your own life, e.g. misunderstandings. This has the advantage of showing that you are human too.

one minute wonder In the right context, a little joke might work without causing offence. For example, in describing how to manage change, you could ask the jokey question "How many people in [insert name of institution or department that resists change] does it take to change a light bulb?" Answer: (in surprised tone) "Change?"

2 **Comparisons.** "The man who stops advertising to save money is like the man who stops the clock to save time" (Anon). "Getting money is like digging with a needle; spending it is like water soaking into sand" (Proverb).

3 **Witty definitions.** The master of this art was Ambrose Bierce (1842–1914), the American journalist and humourist, who wrote *The Devil's Dictionary*. For example: Consult: "To seek another's approval of a course already decided on."

4 **Short quotations.** For example: "To cease smoking is the easiest thing I ever did. I ought to know because I've done it a thousand times" (Mark Twain). Luck: "I am a great believer in luck, and I find the harder I work the more I have of it" (Stephen Leacock). Sincerity: "A little sincerity is a dangerous thing, and a great deal of it is absolutely fatal" (Oscar Wilde).

Introduce some gentle humour to relax your audience.

5.4

Less is more

All too often, we give in to the temptation to add more and more words or slides, but the overall effect is probably to burden our audience with too much information. Keep the focus on your key messages.

It takes time to write a concise, crisp version of a presentation. Go through your draft focusing only on your key message. If you are not sure what that is, work at your draft until you are completely certain about the one main point you're trying to communicate. You will then have some sub-points – some supporting evidence. Be ruthless with yourself; ask: "Does this fit in with my overall aim?" "Does this aspect absolutely have to be included?" If you answer "No" to either or both of these questions, then delete the part that you are considering.

case study Aaron's talk seemed to go on and on, even when he had made all his key messages. He had given in to the temptation to add just one more point... or two... in the hope of persuading more of

"I didn't have time to write a short letter, so I wrote a long one instead" Mark Twain

■ If you are preparing a PowerPoint slide presentation, use only one image per slide. Pare back your headings and captions to a really simple form – you can say more about them than you need to write on the slide. If you have more than six lines on your slide, then reduce.

■ In working through your material, make sure you make it your own. You have been asked to give the presentation, so don't simply repeat all the already well-known facts; give your own personal slant ("I think that possible reasons for the decline in sales include...").

■ At the end, check that your revised sequence still makes sense, that you haven't deleted a key link in your argument or inadvertently excluded the most important reason for an event.

People will thank you if you finish early, but they won't thank you if you over-run!

the audience to his opinion. A friend later said to him, "You finished but you didn't stop." For his next talk, Aaron stopped when he had made all his key points; he quit while the going was good.

5.5

Remember, remember

It can be helpful to learn parts of your presentation off by heart. This means that you don't have to keep looking down at your notes but can maintain eye contact with your audience. It's also good to attempt to learn the names of people in your audience.

Use mnemonics to help you remember parts of your presentation:

■ **Take the first letter of each word to make another word.** For example, on my course on report writing, I teach the basic elements of STAIR: Scope; Target audience; Analysis; Interpretation; Recommendations.

■ **Make up an image or sentence in your mind.** The more unusual or striking the image, the easier it will be to remember. You could also think of a story to link the stages of a process, making up a story with the different elements in order. The more senses you can involve (e.g. smell or sounds) in the story, the more memorable it will be.

Here are a few ways in which you can remember names:

■ **Write down names.** Before a presentation, I draw a seating plan and after greeting individuals as they come into the room, I write their names down on my plan. I can usually get most of them, except when six come at once! During the presentation, I can then refer to their names. One member of the audience exclaimed when I did that once, "How do you do that?" I said, "You told me your name and I wrote it down!"

■ **Associate a characteristic with a name.** If Brenda is blonde, you can think of B for both blonde and Brenda. A friend has two sons: Paul and Leo. Leo is the younger and shorter, so I remember 'L': little Leo. Of course, you don't tell anyone these little secrets; they remain private. You could write down some features using abbreviations.

■ **Alphabetize names in your mind.** This is a personal one as I write dictionaries, but if I have Julie, June and Karen sitting next to each in that order, alphabetizing them is one way of remembering their names. (Beware of coffee breaks when they may not be together, but hopefully you will have learnt their names better by then.)

Use people's names when addressing them. "Thanks, Peter, that's a good point." Beware, however, of overdoing this: to use someone's name every time you speak to them is excessive.

Use mnemonics to learn parts of your presentation in advance and people's names on the day.

5.6

Listen carefully

The art of listening is often neglected as an important skill in communication. Listening to others is vital, especially in presentations that go beyond business and are more personal. Here are seven ways in which you can listen with sensitivity to others.

1 Respect each individual as unique; recognize they have a need deep inside them to express themselves as a distinct person.

2 Focus on the other person; look at them. All too often in conversations, while the other person is talking, all we are thinking about is what we can say in response to them rather than actually listening to them.

case study Rachael led a two-day "Training the Trainers" seminar. At the beginning, she asked the participants to explain why they were attending. One woman, Jane, said that she had been recently promoted to be a trainer, but was feeling daunted because she had the feeling that she had only been chosen because no-one else was available. Rachael

3 Listen to the words other people are saying but go beyond that; notice their tone, facial expressions, be aware of their feelings, when and how they pause; notice too what people are not saying.

4 Understand others. I believe we can only do this effectively if we are confident in ourselves as people rather than constantly being anxious about for example what people are thinking about us.

5 Respect people's privacy and don't delve more deeply than they want to disclose.

6 Listen for cues that people want to disclose more of themselves and respond accordingly, perhaps by a short 'mmm' which expresses the wish to allow the other person to say more or short questions to prompt them to continue.

7 Reflect back, that is summarize in a few words, what the person has been saying. This shows you are really listening and trying to understand. They will soon put you right if you've got it wrong.

Practise the art of true listening.

immediately thought that what this participant needed most was an affirmation of her role. On the second day, she presented Jane with one white lily and the words, "On behalf of the group, I would like to affirm you as a trainer." Jane was visibly moved and later in the feedback session said that it was the most significant part of the course for her.

Be aware of body language

Body language is a very important part of how we communicate. Your gestures and movements will say just as much as your words when you give your presentation. This chapter includes tips and techniques on clothing to wear; the way to stand and move; eye contact with your audience; and control over your voice.

6.1

Dress for success

The clothes you wear are an important part of the image you present. Even in these times of less formality, it is often expected that the person leading a presentation will dress smartly. Moreover, wearing smart clothes often makes you feel good and increases your confidence, so your audience will pay more attention to you.

Here are some guidelines on clothes and personal grooming:

1 It is better to err on the side of being more formally dressed than the members of your audience.

2 If you are in doubt about the dress code that is suitable for your presentation, ask your colleagues what is expected.

3 Wearing clothes that are black, navy blue or dark grey can give you an air of authority. Wearing a bright colour can make you look assertive, creative and dynamic.

4 Wearing pale, pastel colours can make you appear gentle and unthreatening.

5 These days, it is usually acceptable to remove your jacket while speaking. It can be a sign that you 'mean business'.

6 Ties should not be too flamboyant. I recall the time after a presentation when a colleague came up to me. I expected him to comment on my talk but all he said was "I like your tie!"

7 Wear shoes that are clean and smart, practical and comfortable (and not necessarily fashionable).

8 Avoid wearing too much jewellery or heavy make-up. It will look out of place in a business setting.

9 Don't neglect personal grooming. Make sure your hair is clean and tidy, your nails well cut and make-up is appropriate. If necessary use a pleasant deodorant, aftershave or perfume. Make sure it is not too strong.

Wearing smart clothes will increase your self-confidence and give your audience a good impression.

6.2

Stand up and be counted

One of the most important elements of your body language is your posture. It's important that you set a clear message: that you are the centre of attention during your presentation, and that you are confident in what you are saying.

Time and again, research has shown that standing up to deliver a presentation is the most effective way to achieve the attention of the audience. You are best off standing with your feet firmly planted apart. Keep your shoulders back, but relaxed. Don't slouch!

Standing up also should make you more visible to your audience. But you still need to make sure you are visible to everyone in the audience.

case study To begin with Rohid was unsure of himself, so he sat down when leading presentations. He felt insecure and was certain everyone thought he looked foolish when he stood up to speak. However,

"I would rather die standing than live on my knees"

Emiliano Zapata, Mexican revolutionary

1 Check that there aren't any blind spots from where people won't be able to see you.

2 Check that you won't be blocking anyone's view of the screen or visual aids.

3 Check that the lighting is OK – it shouldn't be too dark (which makes it easier for people to nod off) but neither should you have the sun in your eyes.

If you're not sure whether you should be sitting or standing, then you should be standing.

he gradually became more self-confident and learnt that his role as presenter meant he had to stand up. That was expected of him as part of his task of leading the presentation.

6.3

Keep eye contact with your audience

Because you are confident of your presentation, you will not need to look all the time at your notes, so you can focus your attention on members of your audience.

■ **Look at all your audience.** Don't focus on just one section of your audience. Try to make eye contact throughout the audience.

■ **Look out for facial cues.** If members of your audience nod or smile when you look at them, this probably indicates that they are accepting what you are saying. You will also notice if they look puzzled or bored, and if so, you can do something about it by changing the pace or moving to a different aspect of your presentation.

case study In one of Maria's early presentations, she realized that her glasses were ineffective. She is short-sighted, which meant she could focus clearly on her notes, but when she looked up, her perception of the audience was a little blurred. Maria knew that taking off her glasses while looking

■ Persevere if some people avoid eye contact. Do all you can to relax your audience and gradually they will start to feel able to make eye contact with you.

■ Don't stare, though. Don't look for too long at any one individual, as that will make them feel uncomfortable.

■ How to speak one-to-one. When engaged in a seemingly one-to-one conversation, e.g. if someone asks a question, look at that person for some of the time, but also at the rest of the audience so that their attention doesn't start wandering.

■ Dealing with awkward people. When replying to a difficult or hostile question, don't give full eye contact to that person. Give about a quarter of your eye-contact time to that person, and about three-quarters to the rest of the audience. This will enable you to gauge the response of the rest of the audience to the question and your answer.

Make eye contact across your whole audience, even when answering questions from individuals. Don't stare.

at her audience would be distracting for them, so she bore with that experience for the day. But immediately after the presentation, she ordered some varifocal lenses. The result is that both Maria's notes and her audience are now in focus during her presentations.

6.4

Control your voice

Your voice is the single most important tool that you have in giving your presentation. Learn how to use it well to make your presentation effective.

You can learn how to exercise control over your voice as you are speaking. Practise voice control; learn how to breathe deeply – not just raising your shoulders. When you breathe in deeply, you should feel your lower ribs move upwards and air build up in your lungs. Allow the greater force of air to go through the larynx (voice box) at the back of your throat and produce a louder voice.

1 Before a presentation, warm up your voice. Hum; talk to yourself – but make sure no one is around to hear you!

2 Vary the volume with which you speak: sometimes loudly, sometimes softly.

3 Vary the speed at which you speak: sometimes quickly, sometimes slowly.

4 Add a range of tones to your words. Don't speak in a monotone all the time. Sound enthusiastic – your audience will pick this up.

5 Open your mouth wide and move your lips, articulating the words clearly and fully; don't slur syllables.

6 Make sure your voice doesn't drop at the end of sentences. This sounds dull.

7 Emphasize the positive words you want to stress. You could even repeat them to highlight them further.

8 Watch out for the meaningless fillers that we all use: "OK", "you know", "um", "just". Ask a friend to identify those that are your particular weakness. Once during a presentation, I counted how many times the speaker said "um": 114 times in 45 minutes. It is better to be silent than to keep using fillers in this way.

Learn how to breathe deeply and practise voice control.

6.5

Pause for thought

Inexperienced presenters tend to make the mistake of speaking too quickly, rushing through their presentation and giving too much information all at once. As you become more experienced, you can use pauses more skilfully as one of the techniques available to you.

As the presenter, you need to use pauses to keep on recharging yourself to deliver the next part of your presentation. Your audience need pauses too as they listen to you so that they can absorb and digest what you're saying.

one minute wonder Go through your material and identify some points at which you can make a pause for emphasis.

In your presentation, pauses:

■ Are particularly useful after you have just made an important point. They allow the audience to take in what you have just said.
■ Are particularly useful before you are about to make an important point. They prepare the way for something significant to come.
■ Allow you to gather your thoughts, to get your mind ready, when you want to move on to the next point.
■ Mark a break between your points.

Pauses should not be too long, however. It's rather like some of the pieces of equipment at my gym. If I stop on the bicycle, after a while the message on the screen says, 'Pause', but then the machine realizes that I no longer want to continue, and it becomes aware that I have finished. So pauses that are too long may cause an alert member of the audience to call out, "Are you OK?" Long pauses can also lead to tension or drama. So make sure your pauses are intended.

Plan for pauses after you've made important points or when you want to change pace.

6.6

Make a move

It's rather dull for your audience if you deliver your presentation from a static position behind a lectern. Moving more dynamically is a good way to keep people's attention. Here are five golden rules about what to do with your body when you're presenting.

1 Don't hide behind the lectern. Also, don't grip the lectern to steady your nerves. Come out from your safe comfort zone; move out from behind the lectern and walk around the room a little, engaging eye contact with members of your audience.

---

case study George's manager complained that he was too "fiddly" during his presentations, but George wasn't sure what she meant. So she suggested George get someone to record him presenting so he would understand what she was talking about.

---

2 Keep smiling. Smiling will make your audience feel you are relaxed, even if you aren't. It will also relax your audience.

3 Use your hands and other gestures to emphasize your key points, to push points home and to connect with your audience.

4 Don't speak with your back to the audience while looking at the screen or writing on a flipchart; they will pay less attention to you.

5 Avoid distracting habits. Don't play with you hair, jangle keys, play with jewellery or a flip-chart pen, or jingle coins.

Move out from behind the lectern and use meaningful gestures.

Sure enough, as soon as George watched the video of himself, he noticed that every 10 or 15 seconds he would sweep his hair back from his eyes. George was grateful that his manager had pointed it out as he realized many people would find this offputting.

Learn from feedback

As you finish your presentation, you will probably want to invite the audience to raise questions. This can be a good opportunity not only to clarify any points made in your presentation but also to drive home your key messages. You might also ask for evaluation or feedback. There's always room to learn from your mistakes.

7.1

Know when to take questions

As presenter, try not to become too anxious about the idea of taking questions that you might not know the answers to, so making you look foolish. Questions provide you with an opportunity to clarify things that your audience did not fully understand. By following certain guidelines you will worry less about this part of your presentation.

Taking questions during your presentation

If your presentation is informal and to only a few people, you might prefer to accept questions during your presentation. Say at the beginning, "You can interrupt me if you don't understand something and you want me to explain it to you."

This will slow down your presentation, so you will need to remain in control, not get sidetracked and steer the flow back to your plan at an opportune moment. Don't be afraid of saying, "That's a good point – and I'm coming to that in a few minutes." Or: "Let's park that question over here for a while [and gesture with your hands to move an item] and come back to it later."

Taking questions during your presentation means that you can gauge what level your audience is at. I gave one talk and the questioner asked a very basic question that made me realize I needed to adjust the level of my presentation.

Taking questions at the end

If the presentation is more formal and to a large group, then it is more usual to have, say, 15 minutes of questions at the end. Tell your audience at the beginning that they will have the opportunity to ask questions at the end. After your conclusion, pause and then say, "Thank you very much for your attention. I'd now be happy to answer any questions."

If the questions come at the end of your presentation, then make sure you finish on a strong note, with an answer that you have given well. Round off the question-and-answer time by referring to the key messages of your presentation.

Decide if you are happy to take questions during your presentation or if you would prefer them at the end.

7.2

Answer questions well

Having decided when you will answer questions, take advantage of the further opportunity to reinforce the key messages of your presentation. Keep control of this part of the presentation; your performance has not finished yet!

1 Identify likely questions in your preparation and work out your response in advance.

2 Sit down when listening to a question. Stand up as you begin to answer it. (This will give you a little more time to think of the answer.) Taking a drink of water will also give you more time.

3 Listen carefully to the question. Don't interrupt the questioner. Write down key words in their question or as you plan your response and to help you concentrate.

4 Use the person's name in your response, "Thank you, Robert." (See 5.5 about how to remember people's names.)

5 Repeat – or rephrase – the question before you begin your answer. Look at both the questioner and the wider audience as you do so. Repeating the question means that the whole audience will hear the question; it will also clarify it in your own mind and give you time to work out how to answer it.

6 Make sure you give some response to the question that is asked. Do not follow the politician's method, however, of not answering the question.

7 If you don't know the answer to the question, then be honest and say so. You could offer to check out the details and respond to the questioner later or ask a colleague who is present at the meeting and who you know is more expert in that area to respond. Don't try to bluff your way through it, pretending to answer a question when you can't. It will show.

8 Don't allow one or two people to dominate the question time. After responding to one or two questions from a difficult person, say something like: "Perhaps we could hear from others of you with your comments and questions" or "It would be good to hear from a wider cross-section of the meeting." Or you could suggest that the questioner might like to discuss the matter more with you later on a one-to-one basis: "Perhaps we could discuss this further in the coffee break."

Identify likely questions and work out your response in advance.

7.3

Deal respectfully with hostile questions

Sometimes, there are awkward people… people who want to trap you, perhaps show off their knowledge, or disrupt the meeting. How do you respond? Even if the question is put in an aggressive way, it is important for you to try to remain calm and not respond with any hostility. Respect the questioner.

1 In your reply, try to find areas on which you agree and offer these as a basis and then move on from that starting point. For example, you could say, "We're all agreed that the current losses cannot continue and we need to make cuts, but we seem to have different opinions about where those cuts should fall." You could respond, "I wonder what's behind your question. Could you tell us why you're asking that?" Ask the questioner to put his or her question in more specific – rather than general – terms, which you will probably find it easier to respond to.

2 When responding to a difficult question, don't be afraid of stating your position firmly. Hopefully, you will have anticipated some likely questions, including difficult ones, in your preparation and so you will already have thought of creative ways of responding.

3 When replying to an awkward question, give the majority of your eye contact to the rest of the audience (see 6.3). If you maintain eye contact only with the questioner – particularly towards the end of your answer – that person might take it as an open invitation to add another question, which you want to avoid.

4 Don't take any hostility or aggression personally; it is probably directed at a policy or maybe a group of people rather than you individually.

Don't take any hostility or aggression personally.

7.4

Have a focused discussion of your presentation

So you've given your presentation. Perhaps the meeting now has to discuss what you have said and make decisions. It is important that any such discussion centres on the key issues and does not become sidetracked.

■ Don't wait for others to start a discussion: each participant should take an active role.

■ Listen to others. While someone is talking, don't just think what you can say in response; really listen to others' contributions.

■ Focus on the major issues, not minor ones. Keep to the point.

■ Where necessary, challenge ideas, not individuals. Be honest, but not ruthless.

■ Be positive and supportive. Affirm others' contributions.

■ Be willing to change your mind.

■ Where you disagree, be constructive; try to focus on the real issues. Creatively try to find fresh ways of solving difficulties.

It is important that the follow-up discussion should be well led by a good chairperson, who will give a lead, set out the background, keep the discussion focused, make sure that a few people do not dominate, and navigate the discussion through areas of disagreement. A good chairperson will also have discussed controversial issues in advance with key people. Further, he or she should summarize progress, draw conclusions, make sensible decisions and be clear on the next steps.

When deciding on the next steps, it should be clear who is responsible for taking action; and ideally the actions should be SMARTER (see below). They should be recorded in the minutes of a meeting or a follow-up email:

S = Specific. Not vague.
M = Measurable. Can be assessed.
A = Achievable. Possible, within reach, not unrealistic.
R = Relevant. Realistic, not insignificant.
T = Timed. With a specific deadline.

Later, they should be:
E = Evaluated. By others.
R = Reported. To, for example, the next meeting.

When deciding on the next steps, it is important to have clear action points. Think about SMARTER actions.

7.5

Evaluate your presentation

It's important to have some evaluation or feedback on your presentation so that you can know what went well and learn from those parts that worked less well. However well or badly you've done, you can always improve the next time.

Don't just ask a sympathetic colleague, "How did I do?"; seek feedback from trusted friends. (If you are giving feedback, be specific and follow this order: make positive comments to begin with, then negative comments, then finish with positive comments.)

Some of the most helpful feedbacks I have received came from David, the leader of a training organization I worked for: my preparation was good, but the handouts I gave out were far too long.

case study I follow a personal rule not to look at feedback forms until after the first railway station on my way home, 13 minutes out of London. This gives me time to unwind a little. I'm usually pleased

Delegates spent time looking at these so didn't listen to what I was saying. Some points were very helpful but I mentioned them too quickly. I am obviously uncomfortable about being a salesman; I am happier with a "soft-sell" approach.

Sample questions for a feedback form:

■ How knowledgeable was the presenter?
■ How interesting was the content?
■ What was the delivery of the presentation like in terms of pace and timing?
■ Was the presentation pitched at the right level?
■ How helpful were the visual aids?
■ How helpful were the handouts?
■ Would participants recommend others to attend the presentation?
■ How suitable was the room?
■ What was the organization of the presentation like?
■ What specific matters has the presentation helped participants with?
■ How could the presentation be improved?
■ Any further comments?

Get feedback so that you can evaluate the effectiveness of your presentation.

with the feedback forms – the ones that say "You went too fast" are normally balanced out by the ones that say "You went too slowly". I put the positive ones at the top to help my self-confidence.

7.6

Learn from your mistakes

Sometimes things go wrong or work out very differently from what we had planned or expected. The secret is to evaluate your presentation, reflect on it and learn: remember, practice makes perfect!

Over the years, most of the following have happened to me:

■ I've got the timing of my presentation completely wrong - Make sure your most important material comes at the beginning.
■ I lose the interest of the group in the middle of the talk - Have a variety of presentation methods available.
■ Someone walked out in disagreement at what I'd said - Don't take this personally; be professional.

case study Connor has done a one-day presentation on communication for a company for two years running. The first year's event went well: he had good rapport with a group of about 30 in the room. The second year he was confident about offering the same material to a group of 15. What he had not

■ I've forgotten the adhesive… or my notes – Make a note to remember them next time!

■ Key members of the audience are not there or someone unexpected suddenly walks in - Keep going; stay calm.

■ I've not made enough copies of the handout - Quietly ask someone to make further copies, with several extra spare.

■ I've realized my stories or humour are not raising any smiles - Try a different approach and sooner rather than later.

■ I've suddenly noticed my PowerPoints are too densely packed or the font size is too small - Make a note to get it right next time.

■ I've not been able to be heard. A friend once said, "That was a lovely talk, but I couldn't hear a word of what you said!" - Adjust your microphone. Ask if your audience can hear you.

■ The equipment doesn't work - Be patient. Ask for help and explain the situation to your audience. Start without it if necessary.

■ I've had an argument with a friend or colleague just before my presentation - Focus on the present. You've put a lot of hard work into your presentation; don't let anything get in the way of you doing justice to all your preparation.

■ There have been poor handovers between different speakers in a team presentation - Don't let it ruin the rest of the presentation. Do your best to regain momentum.

Beware the common pitfalls and learn how to pick yourself up after a fall.

expected, was the low level of motivation of the smaller group. He had to use all his energy, skills and methods to maintain their interest through the day. The lesson Connor is learning is that every group is different. He needs to be able to adapt his presentation for different audiences.

7.7

Excel in presenting

You are only as good as your last presentation. You need to maintain your skills. You want to be the best, so you need to keep on keeping on. Think of your presentation as part of an adventure – an unusual and exciting experience – go for it!

Some final tips that helpfully make up the word PRICE:

■ **P = Preparation.** Give enough time to planning, writing and rehearsing your presentation. Think clearly. If your key messages aren't clear to you, they won't be to your audience. Don't get sidetracked by all the details and the minor points if you are giving a basic introduction. Stay fresh in yourself. Keep up to date with trends in your own field. Read widely. Take time out to think and work on new ideas and approaches. There is no set formula. Be yourself.

case study For years, in giving my talks I tried to be like two famous speakers who I looked up to: David and James. I read their books, watched their presentations, and even tried to imitate their mannerisms. It took me a long time to realize that I

■ **R = Rapport.** Listen to your audience. Read their responses. If necessary, change tack to keep their interest. It took me a long time to realize that the relationships I had with my audience are crucial. Your audience are not simply listening to a presentation; they are listening to you – a living person – so be real with them! Even say, "I may not look nervous, but I am," if you are – that could defuse the situation.

■ **I = Incisive.** Have something definite to say. Your audience have come to hear your particular approach to the subject, not vague general statements that anyone could express.

■ **C = Control.** Remember you probably know a lot more about the subject than nearly all your audience. They are basically on your side and are not out to attack you! But be flexible. Stuff happens. There can be an unscheduled fire alarm just as you reach your most important point. Or instead of 20 people coming to your presentation, only two turn up. Learn to respond to actual events. If you know your subject well, you should be able to carry it off.

■ **E = Enthusiastic.** Your presentation is an opportunity to impress, not a chance to fail. You can do it!

Remember your PRICE if you want to excel in presenting.

could be myself, that my own distinctive style of presenting and teaching was unique and as valid as each of theirs. The result is that I'm much more relaxed – it's less hard work than trying to be someone else! – and the audiences benefit greatly too.

Jargon buster

Acronym
A word formed from the initial letters of other words, e.g. STAIR for 'scope', 'target audience', 'analysis', 'interpretation' and 'recommendations'.

Alliteration
The use of the same letter at the beginning of a word, e.g., to help as a memorable expression in a presentation.

Allusion
An indirect or implied reference to a well-known event, name, etc.

Auditory learners
Auditory learners like to listen to information and then discuss it with others, listening to what others say, to help them learn.

Bar chart
A bar chart has bars of equal width but with different heights in proportion to the values they stand for. Useful for comparing quantities over time.

Body language
The different gestures, movements and facial expressions that communicate a presenter's meaning, feelings and attitudes.

Eye contact
A direct look between two people.

Flipchart
A pad with large sheets of paper that is mounted on a stand.

Flow chart
A flow chart illustrates a series of steps and is useful to show the stages of a process.

Gantt chart
A Gantt chart illustrates the duration of certain tasks alongside periods of time (months etc.) and is useful for scheduling.

Handout
A document that is distributed to an audience to confirm or supplement a presentation.

Kinaesthetic learners
Kinaesthetic learners like to be active and learn by doing.

Learning styles
The different ways in which people learn. See auditory learners, visual learners and kinaesthetic learners.

Line graph
A line graph shows the relationship between two kinds of information (along the vertical and horizontal axes) and how they vary depending on each other; useful to show changes or trends over time.

Mind Map™

See pattern notes.

Mnemonic

A device such as a mental image or familiar word used as an aid to remember something.

Motivation

The desire and determination to want to do something; inspiration.

Pace

The speed at which a presentation is given.

Pattern notes

A creative diagram that you draw to generate and capture ideas around a central key word. Also known as a Mind Map™.

Pie chart

A pie chart is a circle divided into slices, each in proportion to the quantity it stands for and is useful for comparing data in proportion to a whole, but sometimes difficult for the eye to take in quickly.

PowerPoint

The Microsoft presentation program.

Rapport

A good relationship between presenter and audience.

Video conferencing

A virtual meeting in which participants are linked to one another in real time by means of a video and audio link.

Visual aid

A device such as a PowerPoint or flipchart, or a means of communication e.g. graph or table, that displays in visual form material that is being presented.

Visual learners

Visual learners like to see information in pictures, diagrams, charts, tables and in writing.

Voice control

The power to direct and project your voice, especially as regards how loud, fast and clearly you speak.

Further reading

Bigwood, Sally and Spore, Melissa
Presenting Numbers, Tables and Charts
(Oxford University Press, 2003)
ISBN 978 019 8607229

Buzan, Tony *Mind Mapping* (BBC, 2006)
ISBN 978 0563 520344

Manser, Martin H. *1001 Words You Need to
Know and Use: An A-Z of Effective Vocabu-
lary* (Oxford University Press, 2010) ISBN
978 019 956005 9

Manser, Martin H., with Associate Editors
Pickering, David and Curtis, Stephen *Facts
on File Guide to Good Writing* (Facts on File,
2006) ISBN 978 0816 055265

Manser, Martin H., with Associate Editor
Curtis, Stephen *Facts on File Guide to Style*
(Facts on File, 2006)
ISBN 978 0816 0640412

Manser, Martin H. *Good Word Guide*
(A&C Black, 7th edition, 2010)
ISBN 978-0713677591

Manser, Martin H. and Curtis, Stephen
Penguin Writer's Manual
(Penguin, 2003) ISBN 978 014 0514896

McCallion, Michael *The Voice Book*
(Faber and Faber, 1998)
ISBN 978 0571 195251

Ribbens, Geoff and Whitear, Greg *Body
Language* (Hodder Education, 2007)
ISBN 978 0340 945711

Useful websites

www.martinmanser.com/M/MMTraining.aspx
– for courses led by Martin Manser on
report writing and English grammar

www.capita-LD.co.uk – for courses on
which Martin Manser is an Associate
Trainer leading courses on writing
(Capita Learning and Development)

www.lcc.arts.ac.uk/courses/36844.htm –
for courses led by Martin Manser on
Confident Written Communications and
Business Writing (University of the Arts
London: London College of
Communication)

www.lcc.arts.ac.uk/courses/36832.htm –
for courses led by Martin Manser on
Organizing Effective Meetings, Time
Management and Leadership (University
of the Arts London: London College of
Communication)

www.toastmasters.org – for Toastmasters, group meetings in which participants learn communication skills

www.eureka-tp.com – a website with hints for training trainers

www.trainingzone.co.uk – topical and practical content for corporate training professionals

www.woopidoo.com – a website for motivational business quotes

www.Credoreference.com – a significant general reference resource for learners and librarians with full-text content on all major subjects from outstanding reference works

www.meetingzone.com – the website for MeetingZone, the UK's largest independent conferencing service provider which offers customers a high performance, low-cost personalized audio and web conferencing service

http://images.google.com – an excellent source of an extensive range of images

www.flickr.com – a good online photo-management and sharing application website

www.istockphoto.com – comprehensive library of images that start at low prices

http://office.microsoft.com/en-gb/clipart – website with many images, photos and sounds

www.shutterstock.com – website with images by subscription

www.clipart.com – downloadable images and graphics by subscription

www.BusinessSecrets.net